8–12 YEARS OLD

BENG & FRIENDS

"LEARN ABOUT A" STEM NEW ^ CAREER

Lorna E. Green 2023

D0911306

WRITTEN BY
LORNA E. GREEN

ILLUSTRATED BY
KORI THOMPSON

"LEARN ABOUT A
STEM
NEW ^ CAREER"

where words connect

Beng & Friends: Learn About a New Stem Career

ISBN: 978-1-959811-10-7 (Paperback)
ISBN: 978-1-959811-11-4 (Ebook)

Library of Congress Control Number: 2023903967

Jacket design: Amit Dey
Interior Design: Amit Dey
Illustrations: Kori Thompson

Published by Wordeee in the United States, Beacon, New York 2023

Website: www.wordeee.com
Twitter.com/wordeeeupdates
Facebook: facebook.com/wordeee/
e-mail: contact@wordeee.com
Printed in the USA

Dedicated to the memories of my

Dear Father

Herbert Green
1934-1977

and my son

Abeng Stuart
1978-2017

Gone too soon

CONTENTS

THE SLEEPOVER

A loud tune from one of Beng's favourite artistes blared in his ears. The music woke him from a deep sleep. How silly of him to have forgotten to turn off his automatic wakeup call headset music. He was glad though not to have disturbed the others. His sister, Gillian, also known as Fidge, their cousins, Rachel and Amar, and his friend, Zakai, were visiting for one of their frequent sleepovers and they were still soundly asleep. As the eldest at nine, he was their chaperone of sorts since his older sister Ashley, eleven-years-old, was over at her friend Zoe's for a birthday party and their own sleepover.

At these sleepovers, the kids always slept in the basement game room instead of their bedrooms as they could all be together. The game room was bigger with lots of open spaces ideal for playing video games, watching movies, and relaxing and it was way more fun than bouncing from room to room. On sofas and in sleeping bags no one stirred as he bolted upright. For a moment, Beng did a double take, thinking Fidge was his older sister Ashley. Almost five years apart, Fidge insisted on dressing like Ashley had done at her age. Their Mom had been forced to buy Fidge outfits that were exactly like the ones Ashley had worn when she was seven. *Wow,* Beng switched off the music and got out of his sleeping bag, *they do look alike!*

Beng's dog, Breezy, a playful Labrador-Rottweiler mix, was also asleep in a corner. She lifted her head lazily as Beng walked over to her. Rubbing Breezy's head, Beng hugged her. She was the best dog ever. Breezy had been his birthday gift when he'd turned seven, and she was three. He helped his parents choose her from the animal rescue shelter in town. Though she still looked sprite, she was getting on in age. His mom, Khalilah, on one of their dog talks had once told him, "Dog years are not like people years. For every year you live, a dog ages seven years."

Wow! Beng thought as he approached his best friend. *This means Breezy is thirty-five in human years this year. She still does look young and runs with the same speed as she did last year so that's all that mattered.*

Breezy, stood up, wagged her tail, and licked Beng's hand.

"Let's go for a walk Breezy," Beng said.

Breezy stretched and moved closer to him.

Heading for the stairs Beng looked at the empty pizza boxes, half-eaten fruits, and juice cups scattered on tables, chairs, and the floor. The room was a mess. He'd have to get everyone to pitch in for cleanup when he returned from walking Breezy.

Walking softly to the kitchen, he was careful not to wake his mom who'd stayed up late watching a movie and talking on the phone with his Auntie Dalila. While he wasn't sure what time she'd gone to sleep, he figured it had to have been very late, as it was past midnight when she came down to say goodnight.

Beng took Breezy's leash from the wall rack, attached it to her collar and grabbed her favorite toy from the doggie toy basket.

Impatient, Breezy pulled him toward the door as he saw a bird land on the back porch. The glass door made it very easy to see the porch, the entire lawn, the gardens and all the birds that were always in the yard. When they weren't resting on the porch banister they were chasing insects, eating left over berries and apples dangling from the trees. Beng hurriedly unlock the door inching after Breezy as she crept up on the bird. Breezy was about three feet from the bird, when it flew away. Beng laughed aloud, thinking Breezy should be used to this by now as she did it every morning, and every time the birds escaped. Still Breezy looked annoyed.

The doggie park was a short walk from their home. Nearing the entrance, Breezy started running. Her friends, Bailey, a stately looking Weimaraner, and Boogers, a pint-sized Shih Tzu Poodle, who often acted like he was the big dog in the park, wagged their tails as they saw her.

Beng barely managed to unleash Breezy before the three dogs began romping in the grass with their toys. Deciding against walking over to chat as he planned to leave the park early, he waved to their owners, Marley, and Adam, who lived a block from his house While he stood waiting for Breezy to finish her exercise, he thought about the sleepover.

They sure had fun playing video games, eating pizzas, chips, and candy even though his mom had insisted healthy foods like fruits and nuts be added to the mix.

Beng chuckled as he remembered his cousin Amar's imitation of Beng's dad, and his Uncle Andre. Beng's dad was forever telling them about life when he was young and how they didn't have the opportunities they had today. Beng specifically laughed at the part where Amar, in his best impersonation of his uncle, said, "Now kids, we never had it easy in our day. We grew up in neighborhoods that did not have wide, open playgrounds and weren't as safe as you are today. Yes, we had phones and a few video games but not the smart phones and gadgets you all have now. You must make the best use of the new technologies and gadgets to become your best self. As kids, we were lucky to have had our families close by, so we had tons of good old fashioned fun and looked forward to visiting each other's homes." *Man, that Amar is good at imitating grownups. Maybe he'll be an actor when he gets older.*

Beng's thought was interrupted by Breezy, panting at his feet, her usual cue she was ready to go. Beng leashed her and they started walking back home. In less than two minutes, they were at the front door. Undoing her leash, Beng filled Breezy's pan with clean water, put food in her bowl, and then headed downstairs to organize the cleaning crew.

Just as he picked up the game console to stash it away, his sister Fidge woke up. "What time is it?" she asked, rubbing her eyes.

"Not sure," he said, then looked at his phone. "It's nine thirty."

"Woah. I still feel sleepy," she said. "Maybe we stayed up too late, but it was fun right?" Fidge had watched two movies with everyone else, and then another on her tablet when they'd all fallen asleep. That was the reason, she still felt sleepy.

"Hey, Beng," she said, "last night was so much fun. I thought you and Rachel were going to play Animal Crossing: New Horizons all night. What time was it when you stopped?"

"Not sure," he said, but agreed it was a fun night, reminding her that she was still awake when they packed it in and went to sleep.

"Humm, yes. No wonder I'm tired."

"Don't you go back to sleep. When everyone wakes up, they'll need to pitch in on the cleanup duty before mom comes downstairs," he added.

Fidge groaned, "I didn't make a mess. It was you and everyone else who threw your stuff all over the room." She folded her arms and pouted. "It's not fair that I must help to clean up the mess you all made."

"Mom won't ask for any details," he said, wagging one finger at Fidge. "She's just going to assign chores to everyone."

"Not fair," Fidge insisted. "I am going to talk with Mom about this when she wakes up." Fidge was convinced their mom would listen and not have her help with cleaning up any mess she didn't make. She considered going up to her bedroom to tell her right then. *If I do, then Beng can't make me help*, she thought.

"C'mon, Fidge," he said, "you must help. I just walked Breezy."

"She's your dog," Fidge said nonplussed.

"I know, but we are all down here, so you must help," Beng replied.

Fidge gave him the evil eye, then pretended to go back to sleep.

MORNING CHORES

K halilah opened her eyes, the warmth of the sunlight on her arm.

What day is this? she thought, rolling over to check the time on her phone.

Oh! It's Saturday. The reality of it not being a workday made her relax, giving her the feeling of a 747 gliding to a smooth landing after a long flight. As quickly as her calm set in, she remembered that the house had more than its regular occupants. The kids would need lunch at noon. Last night, she'd promised to make burgers with their favourite trimmings. Though she hoped they would eat leftover pizza, cereal, and fruits for breakfast, a proper lunch is a must.

Oh, well the solitude is over. First, she needed to check on her daughter, Ashley, who was at her best friend Zoe's birthday sleepover. Then she'd run to the market for the ingredients she needed for lunch thinking she'd make something special for Andre. Khalilah wished longingly for her husband, Andre, who was away on business. She was hoping he'd make it home in time for lunch since his earlier text message said he'd be home today, but she didn't need to get him as he planned to take a taxi from the airport.

As she made her way from the bedroom to the bathroom, she was thinking of the kids. How quickly they were growing up. They were beginning to ask questions she sometimes found difficult, and yes, uncomfortable, to answer fully. Did she have such heightened levels of curiosity when she was their age? *I don't think so*, she mused. But they sure have more information coming at them from the internet, social media, and various online applications than she'd had all the way up to college.

The bathroom, bright and airy, was where she enjoyed having her alone time. After completing her routine, she headed down to the patio for her morning exercise. On the way, she realized there was total silence in the house. She thought it curious they were so quiet in the basement too but sensed they were all okay. Still, she peeked down the basement steps and there they were, on their cell phones, furiously typing. Beng, saw her peeking and barely waved. "Hi, Mom," he said then went back to typing.

"Hi Son, is everything ok."

"Yes Mom, everything is ok," he responded without looking up.

Picking up her exercise mat, she went to the patio, turned on the Wi-Fi speakers and punched up her favourite playlist on Spotify, ready to begin her circuit.

Energized from her workout, Khalilah decided now was best to make the short drive to the neighbourhood market. She hoped to get all the lunch ingredients there as the next closest market was in a very congested part of town.

The drive was peaceful and uneventful. She whizzed past homes with little or no signs of life, except the occasional lone person mowing a lawn or tending flowers. She'd grown up only a few miles away from their childhood home. Back then, this area was mostly woods and a few farms. Now, as far as her eyes could see, there were houses, stores, and warehouses occupying the land. The only saving grace was that most of the old oak trees were spared during the construction project and the developer had planted new trees and grass, which made the community look even greener. Her own neighborhood across town where she grew up had also been improved with many amenities. The old supermarket had been replaced by a more modern one filled with fresh fruits and vegetables. There was also a big-box store and clothing stores along the main avenue which made life easier for the residents. Most of the apartment buildings had been refurbished, but not modernized. She felt a lot more could be done to make them look better but alas.

Khalilah pulled into the supermarket parking which was empty. It was 11:00 a.m. on a Saturday morning. Making her way inside the store, she was relieved to see it was also quiet. In a short time, she'd purchased all the items needed for lunch, and was on her way home. The satellite car radio set to her favourite station was playing songs from her teenage years. She snapped her fingers, remembering when she first dated Andre. They had completed high school and were on their way to university, kid-free and carefree. Parties and friendships were all in which they were interested. All summer they'd made beautiful memories, she thought children don't have the opportunity to do these days. She wondered *how these kids would remember their childhood.*

Within minutes she pulled into her driveway, unloaded her purchases, and went to the kitchen to unpacked the groceries.

The children were more active now. From the kitchen, she could hear their chatter in the basement though she couldn't make out their words. After lunch she'd have them clean up the mess in the basement and organize their sneakers which were haphazardly thrown all over the porch. She would make her husband's favourite salad with lunch just in case he made it home. If not, she'd have to eat it herself as the children would only eat very small portions.

KIDS GONE WILD

The basement showed signs of 'kids gone wild' with sleeping bags, leftover pizza, cereal, and fruits everywhere on the floor. Beng looked at everyone, all now awake, chatting and texting away. He reminded them that they all had to pitch in with cleanup. He was annoyed when no one responded, everyone trying to appear occupied.

Amar hummed; his shoulders bounced in rhythm to a song playing on his phone. He then proceeded to send a group text to Zakai and the rest of them, who were sitting next to him. *Have you seen the video of the old people in the funny clothes dancing?*

Yes, I think so, Zakai texted back. *Is it the one where they were dancing and dressed in clothes that look like costumes.* Like the ones he saw in photos of his grandparents and their friends.

Do you think we will look funny like that when we are old like them? Amar responded.

Fidge's eyes were wide open in amusement as she watched the video.

The phone chat was interrupted by a few spoken words. Fingers moved at lightening speed as they typed responses to the lively online discussion of the video, they were viewing on a popular social media site. Several older persons were in the middle of a dance the kids had never seen. Fidge looked up from her phone and laughed, breaking the silence. "Wow! These videos are so, so funny. I wish I could keep them forever. Do you think if we made videos of ourselves dancing, we could keep them for a long time?" When no one answered, she added, "But if we do keep them, would we also look funny to future young people?"

Beng, very annoyed by everyone's lack of response to his request for cleanup, knew he had to do something. As the oldest he would be held responsible, so he decided to act. He got up and stood in front of Fidge to get her attention. When she didn't look up, he yanked off her headphones.

She glared at him, then said loudly, "Leave me alone."

"You all need to help me clean up the mess we made last night," he said, frowning.

"Will you please tell everyone else and stop picking on me. I am not even the one who made the mess," she snapped.

"I will," Beng responded, "but just remember we live here, and mom will make us clean it all by ourselves if we don't do it now, together." Beng then stood on a sofa, waved his arms, and shouted, "We must clean up the mess before mom comes down here. I don't want to get into trouble." As he flapped his arms back and forth, Breezy started barking, and jumping from one sofa to the next like she was expecting him throw a ball or frisbee.

"Okay, okay," Amar said, looking up from his phone. "We will do it now."

The boys gathered pizza boxes and other garbage and dropped them in a nearby bin. Fidge, Rachel, and Zakai also pitched in, and in a few minutes, the room was beginning to look back to normal. When Beng was satisfied that it looked tidy, he rested on the sofa, turned on his phone, and went back to watching videos. As he did, he thought of Zakai's and Fidge's earlier questions.

He then said, "You know the questions you asked about the video are real. When we are older, the young kids will laugh at us because we will be the old people. Young people, who are babies now will be laughing at our clothes and dancing, just like we are laughing at these older people."

"It's true we will get old by the time Geemaa and Granddad get really old, but won't Auntie Kay and Uncle Andre get old before us?" Amar asked.

Beng tried to imagine his mom and dad old like his grandparents, and himself and his sisters as his parents' age. The pictures that came to mind made him quickly snap out of his thoughts. "Sure, they will," Beng answered, "but we have a long time to go."

"You know, my mom told me they didn't have social media and phones like ours when they were young," Rachel chimed in.

"Their lives must have been so boring. I wonder what they did every day without things like social media and video games." Fidge added, looking at Rachel.

"Have you ever seen the big photo albums in Geemaa's house? The pictures are on paper and pasted in this book with clear plastic over them. Can you imagine if they had thousands of pictures like we do on our phones how many books they would need?" Zakai added.

"Where would they store them?" Rachel asked. "They'd have to build a special storage cabinet or even a room."

"Well, I'm sure glad we don't have to do that. All our pictures and videos are stored on our phones and tablets," she continued.

"But," Fidge chimed in, "does anyone know how long we can keep the videos and photographs that we store on our phones?"

"Well, let me think. I'm not sure," Amar said. "The ones we are watching of the old people dancing have been stored somewhere for a long time. They must have had some way to store their videos."

"If we can keep them for a while, that would be great," Zakai said, "But where would we store them so we can keep watching them and not have them deleted?"

"I'm not sure," Amar answered.

"Oh, they can be stored in a cloud, I guess. I heard Cousin Jason talk about a cloud, but I don't know what it really is," Beng answered, then reminded everyone that since Jason was older than them and worked with computers, he would know more about it.

Fidge made a funny face, stood, and moved towards her brother. "Did you say cloud?" Looking out the window at the sky and pointing upward, she said, "Really funny, Beng. I bet Jason was playing a joke on you when he said that. You know he loves to prank us, and here you are believing it. Wow, I must call and tell him this one. You really believe our information from our phones and tablets are stored up there in the sky, in the big white fluffy things that keep moving. Man" She pointed at him, shaking her head in disbelief.

Rachel looked doubtful but urged them to believe that Jason was right. She asked Beng, "Please, tell me how come we can't see the things in the cloud when we look up?"

"You can't," Beng said with an air of authority. "A cloud is not the same thing as the cloud you are looking at through the window. I don't know exactly how it works and who makes it work but I know it's out there and it's not the white things we are seeing in the sky. That's what Jason said, and he is a grownup, so he should know."

"Okay, if it's not the white fluffy stuff, what is it, and how does it work?" Zakai asked. He'd been half-listening obviously missing the explanation Beng had just given. "Never mind. You all look as confused as I am," he said going back to his video game.

ALEXA AND A CLOUD

"Maybe we should ask Alexa," Amar said. "Even grownups ask Alexa things they want to know. Grandad is always asking Alexa about the weather before he goes out."

"Don't forget Mom asks Alexa about her favourite restaurants; if they are open and what are the latest additions to the menus. Alexa knows everything," Fidge added.

"I bet Alexa doesn't know everything," Rachel said, nodding like a wise owl. "There are super difficult questions that I bet you she can't answer, like what is a billion times a billion."

"Come on, Rachel," Amar said. "That's not necessary right now. You can ask that later. Let's just see if she can tell us about the cloud. If Alexa doesn't know, then we will ask Auntie. She will know. She works with computers."

They all nodded in agreement.

"That's a great idea," Beng had to admit.

"So, where is Alexa?" Fidge asked. "Didn't Dad put it in his office? He did complain that we were not being careful and may break it."

"No, he didn't move it," Beng said. "It's right over there," he pointed to Alexa, a gadget shaped like a small music speaker, on a table. Beng walked up to Alexa, hand on one hip, appearing most grownup. He asked, "Alexa, what is a cloud?"

Alexa responded but they were all talking at once, so Beng summarized the response.

"A cloud is water vapors high up in the sky which causes rain."

Fidge jumped from her seat and gleefully pointed at her brother, "See, I told you so!"

As Fidge was speaking, Beng thought the response made no sense. *There must be more information. Jason can't be wrong.*

Just then, Alexa gave another response. "A cloud is also hundreds of computers connected in many places and programmed to communicate with each other. They store information we put in our phones, computers, on the internet, and social media."

Beng smiled, looked at Fidge with an air of victory, and told her in a mocking tone, "You should be patient."

Amar threw both hands in the air. "This sounds very confusing! How can the cloud cause rain and store data? Then, if Alexa is right, the same cloud stores information and causes rain. That's not adding up. Beng, what do you think?"

Beng face scrunched up with impatience. "Amar," he held his chin, and look him in the eye. "I don't think it's the same thing. A cloud that stores the data is not the same as the cloud that causes rain. It's just the same word with two different meanings. Just like when you say Mommy trains at the gym, and she takes the train to work."

"Oh, I get it," A light bulb went off in Amar's head.

Zakai, who was still focused on watching videos, looked up and asked Beng, "When you say the cloud, are you sure you don't mean the sky?"

Beng was now annoyed. Zakai had missed the exchange as well and was asking an unnecessary question. "Where have you been? We have been talking about that and even asked Alexa. Wake up, dude," Beng said, shaking his head in disbelief as he continued, "No, Zakai, it's not … Alexa gave us two answers and I don't think it's the one that has to do with rain falling, so it must be the one about computers hooked up together."

Rachel exited the basement door that led outside and looked up. "So, where is this cloud and what is it made of if it's not the fluffy white things we are looking at?" She was very confused and wanted to watch cartoons, as they were funny, simple, and made her laugh.

"Oh, forget it." Beng said and walked off.

Now engaged in the conversation Rachel asked, "If the other cloud has our information, then someone must have made it and has it at their house." Rachel was picturing a house in a weird, spooky forest, where the computers were kept, with a mean, very old man guarding the door. She dismissed the thought. "What nonsense. If the other cloud is out there, I mean the cloud computers, how come we aren't seeing these computers anywhere in the sky? Ah, ha!" She gestured before anyone could answer, thinking she might just have solved the mystery. "It must be a secret where they are stored."

"Hold up," Beng turned around, holding his head in confusion

"I don't have the answers. Why are you all asking so many questions?" He was very annoyed with himself for not being able to answer them. Maybe if he checked Google, he would get more details. However, he was not sure exactly what he needed to type as the query for Google.

Amar then said, "It's not the rain explanation, but I want to know who owns these computers and why do they call them cloud, which only confuses me more. Couldn't they use another word to describe them? When I find out who owns them, I will write a serious letter suggesting a new name which will clear up this confusion."

"Yes, genius, a new name like what?" Beng glanced at him.

Amar looked puzzled for a second, then snapped his fingers, and smiled as if he just won a prize. "I got it! They could call it Sky Computers."

"Very original, smart one," Fidge smirked. "I can just see you now." She imitated a grownup male voice. "Madam, you named the cloud wrong, why did you do that? Don't you know you are confusing kids and that's not nice. Just call it Sky Computers." "I bet they wished they'd thought of it first," Amar seemed pleased with his brilliance.

Everyone laughed. Finally, Zakai, who had put away his video game, looked at Fidge and said, "First, it could be a Sir he could be writing to and second, Sky computers or not, is this cloud smart enough to know when you need the information after you put it there?"

Fidge chimed in. "If this sky cloud holds videos and photographs, where does all the other information we type, such as school projects and text messages get stored? I am going to call Mom," she said, hitting the speed dial and speaker on her phone. As she did, Beng took her phone and held it high in the air.

MOM KNOWS ALL

In the kitchen, Khalilah grabbed her ringing phone. Her husband must have landed. Peering at the screen she realized it was her daughter, Fidge, calling. Thinking something was wrong, she blurted, "Is everything okay?" She was expecting a complaint, or worse, a report of something broken or to hear someone crying.

"Nothing's wrong, Mom" Beng responded. "We need to ask you a question. We were, just talking about where all the information we put in our phones and computers gets stored after we press send."

"Also, Auntie Kay, his shortened name for his aunt Khalilah, we need to know when we get information from the internet, where that information is coming from," Amar's voice was loud, as if he was shouting over Beng's shoulder.

"Amar?" Khalilah asked, to be certain.

"Yes," Fidge answered, speaking loudly near the phone.

Then Amar continued, "Who works to make this happen? Beng told us he heard Jason talk about a cloud; we don't know what it is exactly as Alexa gave us two answers for the word cloud."

"Alexa said that a cloud holds all the information we type on our phones and put on social media. Is that true?" Rachel added.

Fidge yelled over Rachel, "Mom, Beng really doesn't know. Alexa is very confused about the cloud. How can the cloud be computers and cause rain at the same time?"

Khalilah laughed and shook her head. "Amar, I'll try to answer but first, tell me, how did this need to know about clouds come up and Fidge, why are you using your phone to ask me these questions when we are in the same house? I am in the kitchen. Come on up and we can discuss this over lunch which is ready. After lunch we can visit the computer store in the mall for more information."

Fidge shouted to the others, "Lunch is ready. Let's go!"

Khalilah heard the children coming before she saw them and was thankful no one hurt themselves in their rush to the kitchen. She instructed Beng and Fidge to set the placemats on the porch table, and the others to get the dishes and utensils they needed for lunch. The kids were a curious bunch she thought and was glad the silence she'd observed earlier was not inactivity. Most children their ages were not just making voice calls, texting, and playing video games, they were using the technology, cell phones and tablets to socialize, research, and communicate. So different from her experiences three decades before when she was a preteen but excited to see their interest in scientific stuff. Back when she needed to learn about things that seemed mysterious and complicated, like the personal computer, DVDs, and cell phones, she would have asked her friends or grownups. She too recalled trying to understand personal computers and networks, wondering how they passed information around but there were few experts back then as the internet was new and still a mystery to everyone. Accompanying this new technology development were new interactive gadgets, such as video games and cell phones, which were at that time, revolutionary developments in technology. This generation had more complex technologies some of it still mind bending even to her who was a computer engineer. Thankfully they could now ask and get answers to difficult questions instantly from the various technologies, connected by the internet.

The kids who were in the kitchen chattering and complaining about each other and the events of last night filed out onto the patio.

"Oh, no, you don't," Khalilah said realizing they'd not washed up for lunch. "Leave your cellphones on the kitchen counter and head to the bathroom," she insisted.

The kids rolled their eyes in jest, answering in a loud chorus, "Okay, Mom . . . Okay, Auntie."

Within minutes, they stood in front of her with their hands in the air, fully washed and dried. Breezy sprawled out on the rug, looking as if she wanted nothing to do with anyone or anything anymore, did not move.

Fidge told her mom that she'd being unfairly treated, by being forced to clean up a mess she didn't make. "Mom, can you imagine I ate some pizza, then put my napkin and plate in the bin, but this morning Beng insisted that I help with tidying up. Please tell him it was not fair."

Khalilah pretended to ignore her, but she continued, "Mom, don't you think I am right that it was unfair that he did that?" she pleaded for her mom to side with her.

"Oh, Fidge," Khalilah said, hugging her, "it's not that it's unfair. Beng has no way of measuring who contributed exact amounts of the mess, so it's only fair he asked everyone to pitch in and help. As the saying goes, 'Many hands make heavy work light.'"

Fidge reluctantly said, "Maybe, I guess."

"Great," Khalilah replied.

Rachel whined, putting in her own complaint. "I only got three slices of the special pizza I ordered." She spread both hands. "Everyone thought it was the best of all the pizzas. Auntie," she continued, "I did ask them when we were ordering if they wanted veggie toppings like mine and they all said no. They always do this, and I don't like it. Now I am hungry because they all ate more than me last night."

"Don't worry, sweetie," Khalilah said. "There is enough lunch for everyone. You will be fine."

"Okay, Auntie, I sure hope so."

Amar told his aunt how noisy they were, which made it hard to concentrate on his game, but Zakai teased that it couldn't be true as he was able to play with him and win. "Amar is just trying to make excuses," he said.

Amar rolled his eyes insisting it was not so. "How could I concentrate with all that noise? Try me again and see if I don't beat you this time."

LUNCH AND A CHAT

Putting the food on the table she again wished Andre were home. He would have enjoyed this exchange and be excited by the kids' curiosity. Her phone rang again, and as if he knew she missed him, this time it was indeed Andre.

"Hey there, I was just thinking about you," Khalilah said.

"That's nice. My presentation went well." He went on to tell her about the engineering project he presented. "It was well received. I'm really happy about that. I'm heading to the airport now, so I was just checking in. How are the kids?"

"They have been very quiet and well-behaved."

Laughing, Andre asked, "Are you holding them hostage?"

"Not me," she responded, "but curiosity. I'll tell you about it when you get here. We're just about to sit down to lunch and I get to answer questions about how things get stored on computers and the internet."

"That's fantastic. Thinking children. I love it!"

Khahilah shared some details of the questions the children were asking and asked his opinion on the best way to respond.

"Don't make it too simple but also not too complicated," Andre said. "Most importantly, you don't want to confuse them."

"Preteens today are not the same as preteens of decades ago. It's difficult to give them vague answers especially when they can immediately fact-check things using Alexa, Siri, Google, and other search engines. I'm grateful for all the online help as they are much more inquisitive on a wider range of topics. But I'm glad they asked. Makes for good lunch conversation."

"That it does," Andre agreed.

They said goodbye and hung up. It was now past noon. Khalilah always preferred dining on the outside porch when the weather permitted, and it was a beautiful day. When the children were all seated, she tipped, looked over at them and asked, "So, why do you all need to know about a cloud?" She liked the fact that they were curious about this aspect of technology, which was now part of everyday life. "But," she continued, "instead of coming to speak with me upstairs, you called me, even though we are in the same house." Maybe the kids would follow in hers and Andre's footsteps and become engineers.

"Before you answer let me give you some advice. In the future, in a situation like this, I suggest that you please ask me in a calm voice from the top of the stairs, and not shout from the basement over your phones. Let's use those phones for the right reasons. Okay? And do so without shouting!"

Rachel looked pleading at her Aunt. "Can we please say grace and start eating, before we talk about the cloud, Auntie?"

"Wow," Beng chimed in, "didn't you eat fruit and cereal this morning?"

"Yes," she said, "but I'm still hungry. Clearly, I am hungry because you all ate most of my pizza."

"Really?" Amar said, in a tone suggesting he was not pleased with her accusation. "We ate most of your pizza? I remember you eating three slices and telling us that you were full."

"Of course, I was full at the time," she replied. "But I didn't say or mean you should take the leftovers. I didn't eat your leftover pizza, so you all shouldn't have eaten what I left in my box. "Greedy," she muttered, under her breath.

The others laughed. Fidge tried to soothe her ruffles. "We won't do that again, Rachel. Next time we'll ask if you are finished before we eat your food. Better yet, you and I could just hide the leftovers," she suggested, smiling mischievously.

Rachel rolled her eyes, ignoring her.

Cross chatter about who ate what made the table noisy. Khalilah asked for silence and proceeded to say a quick blessing for the food and family.

The kids were all excited as Khalilah delivered as promised. The lunch consisted of burgers, both meat and veggie, which looked scrumptious. The vegetables with dip were placed next to the sweet potato fries and salad.

Fidge looked up, "Mom, you remembered that Rachel must not eat meat?"

"I remembered and there are many choices for her. There is something for everyone and dessert is a surprise," Khalilah replied.

Khalilah decided to spend a few minutes recapping the previous night's group entertainment activity. She asked about the movie they'd watched and was pleasantly surprised by the way they'd made their choice. Zakai had suggested they each put two names in a hat, one with the name of their favourite movie and the other of a new one they wished to see.

There was a brief debate as to details.

"What if two people choose the same movie, would they get a chance to put in a second one?' Khalilah asked. Then Rachel had suggested, "We'd put the suggested one in and have both persons agree on a second one to be included."

Khalilah was truly impressed with these young people. "So, let's use the same process for the movie we'll watch later. If there's a tie, I'll then pick the winner from the lot." To her surprise, there was no disagreement. Everyone agreed they'd watch the movie she picked.

She had barely finished speaking when Rachel offered to show her the video of the old people dancing. Khalilah was not sure which video they were watching.

What Rachel showed her to Khalilah's amusement, was familiar and funny. The people were closer to her parents' age and were dressed in 1970's-styled clothes. Tight-fitting pants with bold stripes and bright colors which flared from knee to ankle. The shirts and blouses were equally as colorful, but baggy on both the males and females.

As she watched them dance the Funky Chicken, Khalilah couldn't help laughing. Pointing to the video, she said, "That could be Geemaa and Granddad. That's exactly how they dressed and danced when I was a kid. Where did you find this? It's funny.

It's like we entered a time machine and went back at least forty-five years."

"Is a time machine a real thing, Auntie?" Zakai asked.

"Not yet, dear. It's only in movies. There was a popular one when I was a teenager called *Back to the Future*."

Rachel then asked her aunt, "Do people still dance like that and do you know how to do it?"

"Most certainly," Khalilah said.

Rachel then held her phone in the air while moving her arms, imitating the moves on the elderly dancers as she snapped her fingers, she announced that she could show her Auntie the dance.

"Great, Rachel. let's see you do it," Khalilah said.

Rachel pulled the chairs and tables back a bit, so she would have space to move. The others groaned, but Khalilah said she thought it was a good idea, as they would see the dance moves better. Fidge and Zakai also pushed back their chairs saying they wanted to join in, as they hurried to the kitchen, to get their phones so they could snap some pictures and even make videos.

"Great. Looks like we have a party going here," Khalilah said.

"If we can call these old songs party songs," Amar grumbled under his breath while smiling.

Khalilah laughed, letting him know that they were called oldies, and are lots of fun. At parties with Geemaa and her friends there was a lot of dancing and laughter.

She added, "Let us watch the dancing then finish our discussion on the cloud."

"So, are we having a competition here?" Beng asked. "I thought we came to talk about the cloud, not to dance."

"Oh, be a sport," his mom said, as she connected her phone to the Bluetooth speaker on the counter. "We just ate, so let's have some fun and exercise," Khalilah added. "The most important thing to is to get the same music they have on the video, so we can get the moves right." The song on the video was "Funky Chicken" by Rufus Thomas. *A true gem*, she thought, standing with her legs apart, ready to go. She paused the music.

Rachel, Fidge and Zakai joined her. Beng and Amar rolled their eyes, looking on.

"Stand like a bird, put your hand under your arm pits, bend your knees slightly and stick your head out. Yes, just like that. You must feel like a chicken," Khalilah instructed. She restarted the music, and the song filled the room from the booming speaker. "Now, try moving your hands in and out like you are flapping them, then move your feet together and apart. Also move your head in and out. All at the same time," she said, smiling.

"O-M-G! This is hard," Fidge whined, "How can you move so many parts of your body in different directions at the same time?"

"You are right," Rachel added. "It is harder to do than it looks on the video."

"Well," Zakai said, "so much for this, Auntie, you can show them without me participating."

"Sure, relax, old man," she teased.

Khalilah continued dancing as Fidge, and Rachel tried keeping up while looking cool. Khalilah drifted to memories of the rent parties her parents used to have in their two-bedroom walkup. It was small–too small–she thought for the family of five. But it worked, and she was proud of her parents for their hard work, love, and support. Those parties were held for two reasons. One was to collect a small fee for entrance, which helped to pay the rent, and the other was for the whole family and friends to meet and have fun. Even though kids were not allowed to stay up past midnight, they too had lots of fun. Her parents, bless their "Funky Chicken" dance, were the biggest cheerleaders for her brothers, sister, and herself. Like her, both her brothers and sister were also doing well in their careers and personal lives.

Khalilah felt Beng tugging at her, "Mom, are we having a party here or are we going to discuss the cloud?"

"YES, YES!" Khalilah responded, realizing she had been dancing for a while. "Of course! We are going to have the discussion. I was having so much fun. Thanks for showing me this. It sure brought back memories."

"Like what, Auntie?" Amar asked.

"Well, let's save that for another time. Enough about the "Funky Chicken" and memories for now."

OLD VS NEW

K halilah wanted to continue dancing but saw Beng and Amar looking bored. Breezy was in the corner snoring faintly. She sat down, gesturing to Zakai, Fidge and Rachel to do the same.

She began, "When you called from downstairs, you said you all were confused because Alexa gave two different meanings for the cloud."

"Yes, that's why we came up to you," Beng replied.

Fidge chimed in, "Yeah, that and lunch."

Khalilah continued, "Alexa is right. Both definitions are correct. The same word has two different meanings."

"Mom," Beng said, "I did tell them it's possible and I used the example of the word train. I told them you train in the gym and take the train to work." Scratching his head, he said, "It's a homonym, right, Mom?"

"Yes, son, you sure are correct."

"Now, for the purpose of this discussion, we'll be discussing the cloud that means a network of computers. It is the correct

one when asking about how files are stored. You all know what a network is?" Khalilah asked.

"Yes, we do," Beng volunteered, then explained, "Well, I know Dad has all our computers connected by cables and Wi-Fi that allow us to pass information to each other in the house and print when we need to."

"Yes, that, in a nutshell, is a network. So now imagine connecting thousands of computers by cable and wireless networks all over the world, that can send information and allow people to talk with each other quickly over the internet," Khalilah continued. "Do any of you remember the telephones that are at your grandparents' homes?"

"Yes," Amar said, "they are funny looking. You can't walk around with them because they are big and connected to the wall. There is also a cordless one, but it too is big and clumsy to hold. They are only for talking, nothing more."

"You are right," Khalilah agreed. "When I was a teenager, we did have cell phones, but they looked totally different from the phones we now have. They were very big and clumsy to hold."

"What do you mean big and clumsy, Auntie?"

"When they were invented a few decades ago they were large, and heavy like a small brick. They also were very expensive and did not become affordable for a long time. Growing up, I did not have my own phone nor video terminal. Daddy didn't either."

"Mom, how did you call home if you were out, and how did you do your homework without a tablet?" Fidge asked.

"Well, I had to use a payphone, when I was not at home, and if we needed help with our homework, we would call friends."

"Payphone? What is that? Did the phone pay you?" Fidge asked as she looked at her mom in disbelief.

"No, silly, I put coins in the phone to use it. Sort of like a vending machine."

"You mean the machine would give you a phone when you put the money in and then you use the phone and put it back or keep it?" Zakai chimed in.

They sure were curious. Khalilah needed Google to show them pictures of a phone booth. She asked them to type 'picture of phone booth' in their search bar and press images. They all gasped, then said "Wow!" almost in unison, as images of telephone booths, commonly used up to early 2000, appeared.

"This looks like these phones have their own house," Zakai said.

"He's right, Mom," Fidge added, "Why is the phone in a big box? Was it big and heavy?"

"Well, I do feel older than my age today," she said, as she looked at them playfully. "The phone itself wasn't very big but those boxes or houses were used to protect the phone from rain and sun and gave the person using it some privacy. It had to be big enough to hold a grownup and able to have a door which could close. Now we have cell phones and computers we don't need those big phones. We can discuss the technology that makes phones smaller another day but all the communication we now have come from this connectivity technology. You won't fully understand it but in school, if you take science courses, you'll learn about it." She glanced at their puzzled faces. Then continued, "Let us talk about the information storage, like the video we just watched to find out more about where its kept and who looks after it. When I say look after it, I mean who takes this large amount of data or information and organizes it so we can see it in the order we want, when we want."

"One minute, Auntie, are you saying someone must work with the computer, video game and our cellphones to organize the information for us?" Amar asked.

Khalilah debated with herself, how much concepts and details she should share, realizing she could possibly confuse the children. "I'll try my best to give you a brief description and when I'm finished, if it is not clear, then we'll continue the discussion when we visit the computer store in the mall. Okay, let's start with the storage of information and data in 'a' cloud, not 'the' cloud in the sky. Then, I will tell you about a new career, which is for people working with cloud information, called big data engineers."

She continued, "Each cell phone, video game, and gadget like Alexa and Siri, all operate using computer and software applications. The information that is created when we ask questions, play games, type documents, send voice notes and text messages, is converted into computer language, and stored on the computers. It's like a circle; you type and speak information into the computers and applications. They then process your data and return it to you when needed." They were all still confused. She reminded herself to be clear and simple in her explanations.

"Wow! It really seems like a circle and is a lot to remember," Zakai said.

"Mom, are you really saying everything we do with the gadgets and computers are stored somewhere?" Beng asked.

"Correct," Khalilah smiled, "but let us not get ahead of ourselves."

She suggested, they think of the apps on their phones, gadgets such as Alexa and Siri, information on their computer, video games, and all their other computer-based activities that are there to use from the time they wake up until they go to sleep.

"Whether you talk or type, the information you enter or delete is already stored on another computer called a server. The information from the server is connected to other computers in a network so technically it is not deleted."

Beng looked at her, shaking his head in disbelief. "That's a lot to imagine, Mom. I talk to Alexa all the time and I play games by myself and with my friends online and that's just a small amount of the social media and texting I do every day."

Rachel raised her hand, looking puzzled, "Auntie, are you saying everything we do on the apps, and download on our phones and computers is stored somewhere?"

"That's right," Khalilah replied, "and if you think that is a lot, then think of the millions of people who are doing that, all day, every day, around the world."

"Wow!" Zakai laughed. "That's like a kazillion people! Auntie, can you write a kazillion?"

Khalilah laughed then assured him, "That is not an exact number. Gazillion is the same as kazillion and they both mean very, very large but they do not represent an exact number."

Rachel was not sure how kazillion can be very, very large but is not a number. "How can that be?" she asked.

"It's only a description, not an exact number," Khalilah explained.

Still searching for a simple way to explain things, Khalilah suggested, "Let's talk about some examples of how large the amount of data can be on a network and across the whole world?"

They all seemed very attentive.

EXPLORING THE WORLD

There was strong wind and across the yard and porch. Some toys were being blown about. The plants in the flower beds swayed in the breeze. As the skies were clear with no hint of rain, Khalilah decided to continue. "Whatever we think it is, let's agree it's a lot. Let us take one example which I am sure you are very familiar with going online to buy toys and clothes. All that information is stored on computers all around the world. The computers that store the information are all linked together, but many are in different places."

"Like how many?" Fidge asked.

Khalilah thought for a bit, then answered, "From say ten to several thousands. Think of very large companies like Amazon, TikTok and Uber. Their applications will need thousands of computers all across the world. Just think of all the people watching videos, ordering food, clothes, and toys at the same time all over the world."

Khalilah had an idea, "Let us compare shopping online, with shopping at the mall. They are similar but are also different. At the mall, you have items you can touch and feel. On the computer, you see pictures of the items you select, and have information on how to order and pay. If you decide to purchase an item at the mall, you take it to a computerized machine for self-checkout or a cashier will process your purchase. Either will take your money and give you a receipt. On the computer, you agree to purchase, then pay with a credit card. The item purchased will then be delivered to the address you entered or is collected where it is purchased. In both cases, there are computers that receive and store the information from your purchase."

Beng stood up and walked over to his mom on the opposite side of the table. "This is too much information, Mom. All we asked about was some old videos and the cloud."

"Oh, come on, Beng," Amar said. "We need to get the full, grownup explanation so we can explain the cloud to everyone at school."

Khalilah continued to explain, using the example of playing video games at home and at the arcade.

The kids all brightened up at the mention of games.

She asked them, to think of the arcade, and the games they played there. "You pay for tokens and are given set times for playing each game. When you play on your gaming consoles at home, you have already purchased the game and can play whenever you wish. In both instances, the computer stores information on the games you play."

"So then why do we have to go to the mall, Mom?" Beng asked.

"Well, do you want to stay indoors all day and night? Don't you like going outdoors and seeing your friends and other people?" she asked in a matter-of-fact way.

"Plus, when we go to the mall, we get Cold Cup ice cream, and we can't taste that on our computers," Zakai added confidently.

"True, we can't taste it," Beng told Zakai, "But you can order Cold Cup online, on Uber Eats, and a delivery service will bring it to you."

"Let us get back to the part where the videos like the "Funky Chicken" dance are stored and available to us," Khalilah urged. "Remember the video was recorded a very long time ago and you are still able to retrieve it from storage. We also discussed the many other types of information that are stored on computers. The computers that are linked in a network by wireless connections and computer cables can communicate with each other, and when asked will give us the information we request. We call those large numbers of computers connected to each other around the world, a cloud."

"Why a cloud?" Fidge asked, "Amar was right. The people who make these things want to confuse us?"

"Because the signals needed by the computers to do their work travel through 'space.' The computers receiving the signals are not in the sky but are in buildings all around the world. "We pass one of these buildings every time when we drive to Geemaa."

"Where Mom?" Beng asked. "I have never seen it."

"It's because it doesn't have a large sign. It's the big one-story gray building next to the Farmers' Market." The area was mostly open fields, farms, and small shops. The rolling hills and greenery made for a very picturesque, postcard-like view.

Beng frowned, as if trying to remember the area his mom had mentioned. "Is it the building near the antique store?" When she shook her head, he tried again. "Is it the one that is way back from the road and has a huge sign with a symbol that looks like a lightning strike?"

She nodded.

"Wow! I *do* know where it is, but I would never dream there are lots of computers in there and that it's a cloud." He paused for a moment, thinking. "So, the cloud is on the ground. Man, that's crazy!"

Amar snickered, "I'm going to start a petition to change the name. No way you can call a building a cloud. The people who did this sure didn't think that part through."

Fidge stood and asked, "Then it is computers talking to each other?"

"Yes, but they do so in computer language," her mom replied.

"Who looks after these computers and the networks?" Rachel asked.

"Good question," Khalilah responded. She told them there are persons whose jobs it is to look at, review, and analyze all the information that's written and spoken into computers, other devices, and applications. She also repeated that the information is also called data.

They all looked on attentively, as she continued, "Yes, it is real. These people are paid well to do this job. Remember I mentioned the big data engineer earlier?"

"But, Auntie, if they are looking at the data while we speak and type, isn't that nosy and don't we need to be extra careful when we write and speak on our devices?" Zakai asked, looking annoyed.

Khalilah thought about how much the privacy of persons using the internet, and the ownership of the data created by people using the internet have now become daily debates in the society. She also wondered if there will be any resolution of these issues before these children become teenagers. *Would users own the data they input and create, or would the network and application owners have ownership?* For the time being, however, she had to continue finding simple ways to explain to these smart children the complex technologies which were so integrated in their lives.

She smiled and responded, "Yes, you better be careful. There is so much information created every day that there are persons now who have careers sorting and making sense of what is called raw data."

"Raw data? Right," Beng chimed in sarcastically. "Soon you will be telling us about cooked data."

Khalilah looked at him and reminded herself that there were times as a kid when she said similar things at her family dinner conversations, sometimes annoying her dad. He would take a deep breath; then patiently explain things she and her siblings did not understand.

All the kids look at her quizzically.

Khalilah answered, "No. It's just a description of the data that is typed or voiced in the format that the application is set to receive. Of course, this format may be different in each application. It–the various forms of data–need to be reviewed and put in order and in common formats by people called software engineers. Raw data is then used for analysis and reports. I guess you could call the sorted data 'cooked'."

She smiled and continued, "We could say raw data has not been worked on by the computer professionals, and cooked data means what happens after they make it common and usable for all persons who need it."

All the kids shook their heads in agreement, as if they understood, then Amar reluctantly said, "Kinda makes sense."

"Okay, Mom, so the person 'cooking' the data takes a plane flying through the water clouds and then go to all the computer clouds in different places to get the raw data to cook it?" Fidge asked, as she looked out the window, at the clouds.

"Wow!" Mom responded. "That's cute but, no, my dear. They do not have to take a plane to get the data. Remember the cables I mentioned earlier?"

Fidge, not about to give up, continued, "Please explain how it is done and who tells them to do it? Why can't we do it? Aren't we the ones who put the data in, and don't we know how to use a computer?"

"Sorry, hon, it's not that simple. The activities you describe are complex. Many grownups working in this field have had lots of training. Many go to a university or college and study information systems for years to get a degree in computer science."

"Oh, no! That's a long time," Beng said.

" Yes. It can be. These persons," Khalilah said, "Are hired by companies as big data engineers."

"Oh, my head hurts." Beng said.

"Do you all want me to continue?" Khalilah asks.

"Could we take a water and bathroom break first?" Amar suggested.

"Can we add cellphone to that too?" Fidge chimed in.

"Yes, but please do not start playing games or start calls you know will take a long time. There are a few chores to do before we go to the mall and go see your grandparents. Before you do all that, please pick up all the sneakers thrown around outside and put your bikes in the garage," Khalilah instructed.

"Okay, Mom," Beng said. "We will take care of it now."

Beng and Amar walked to the far side of the porch, looked at their sneakers, then at each other.

"Did we really leave these here?" Amar asked.

"Guess so," Beng replied.

In the bunch was Beng's prized Yeezy's he couldn't believe he'd so casually flung off. *It was a miracle Mom didn't trip over them on her way to the market,* Beng thought.

Rachel, Zakai and Fidge rushed to the kitchen and got their phones. Rachel got in a quick game imagining her game moves being stored on computers somewhere and watched over by big data engineers. It seemed creepy to her. She would have to be more careful about the things she typed and said on her phone in the future.

Zakai called his dad. As the phone started ringing, he imagined his voice travelling over cables or in space and being stored in computers. *Oh, man! There are people who can tell everything I am saying to Dad. I must be careful with my words,* he thought.

His dad answered, asking, "Are you okay?"

Zakai assured him everything was fine then gave an update on the discussion they'd been having with Auntie Kay. "I'm still really confused Dad, but I learned one thing, I must be careful what I say, and type and I'll never see a cloud the same way again without thinking of "raw" and "cooked" data.

His dad laughed, saying, "I'm sure it will get clearer when Auntie Kay is done explaining. Be sure to ask questions if you not understand."

"I will, Dad," he said, then hung up.

Fidge was on the phone, in the hallway, with her best friend, Shane, talking about the upcoming concert at the arena. She wanted to know if his dad had agreed to take them as her mom and dad would be away.

"Dad did say yes. But he needs to speak with Auntie Kay and Uncle Andre first."

"I already asked them," Fidge replied. "They said if your dad takes us, its fine."

"Okay then. Seems like we will be going," Shane responded then said, "Have to go Fidge, later."

Fidge was very pleased. She skipped down the hallway, smiling, convinced they would attend the concert.

Back in the kitchen, Khalilah's cellphone rang. It was Andre. He must have just landed; with only carry-on luggage it would take a few minutes for him to be out of the airport. With no rush-hour traffic, the cab would get to the house in about forty minutes. When she answered, he said, "I am here. The airport is a bit crowded, but I should be home by soon."

"We are on a break from our most curious discussion. Sorry you are missing it, but I'm sure you will soon get your turn at another topic. They are genuinely inquisitive and funny. There is an innocence to their questions which I find entertaining. I think they are all going to be scientists. We were going to go to the Mall and to see gramps, but we'll wait for you to get here. "

"Sounds great," Andre replied. "I will be there as quickly as I can. Love you. See you in a bit."

Beng walked in the kitchen as his mom hung up her phone. "Mom, have you heard from Dad? Isn't he supposed to be coming home today? I want him to show me how to tighten the bicycle rack because that is the reason the bikes are on the floor. It's loose. Last time we tried, he did say we needed a special type of tool to tighten the screws. If I knew which one it was, then I would get it at the Mall and surprise him."

"You know, son, he just called from the airport to say his plane has landed, and he will be home shortly. Let's wait until he gets here then we can sort that out. Let's get started on the rest of our discussion."

Beng agreed, as they had other things to do and the break was already thirty minutes.

"I will get them, Mom," he volunteered and yelled, "Hey everybody, Mom is ready!"

Khalilah tapped his shoulder jokingly and said, "Can you say that any louder?"

"Sure, Mom, should I show you?" he laughed.

"No, thanks, we are all good here, and surprisingly my ears are still fine."

DAD IS HOME

The kids were back on the patio seeming eager to continue. Before they got started, there were a few questions about personal matters. Fidge wanted to know if Mom had spoken with Uncle Grayson about taking her and Shane to the concert at the arena.

"Not yet. I'll do so before the weekend. One more thing I must remember to remember," she said laughing.

"Oh, by the way, Auntie," Amar said as he turned to face her.

"Did you ask Mom if I could go with you and Beng to the laser show next week? I asked her, but she is waiting on your call."

"Most certainly will, Amar. Please do me a favor and remind me tomorrow."

"Thanks a million, Auntie Kay," he replied.

Khalilah sat at the table and tried to recall where they'd left off before the break. "Oh, yes!" she said, "we were discussing some of the different types of data that is collected by these trained persons from our phones, computers, social media, and the internet. We also talked about the computers that process data in a network then transmit this information to us. I know there is some disagreement on calling these computers 'a cloud,' but let us agree we must use that name for now." Thinking how many young persons were using social media to organize change in various causes globally, Khalilah didn't doubt these kids could petition a name change if they tried. But she wouldn't encourage them to do so at this time.

Since all plates and serving dishes were almost empty, she decided to serve dessert.

Khalilah went to the kitchen and returned with warm apple pie and three flavors of ice cream.

"Yippee!" shouted Fidge, "My favourite! Can we have seconds? Mom, you should have told us this was dessert and not make it a surprise. I wouldn't have eaten so much."

"That's exactly why I didn't, my dear," Khalilah replied, reminding them they needed to finish their lunch before starting dessert.

"We understand, Auntie, but you know your apple pie is the best and the ice cream from Cold Cup is to die for, so we can't help ourselves," Amar said, as he winked at her.

"Thanks for the compliment, my dears, but I won't be any more generous with your portions if you praise me," she teased.

Beng jokingly asked his mom if the ice cream was low-calorie, as he was allergic to sugar.

"Beng, you are truly hilarious. Maybe we can send you on a comedy tour," Khalilah suggested.

Khalilah heard a key in the front door and Andre's voice announcing he was home. Could forty minutes have gone by so fast, Khalilah looked at her watch. "We are all on the back porch, dear," she shouted.

"Mom you should not shout" said Fidge and Beng as they bolted to greet him.

"Hey, everyone," Andre laughed as he hugged his kids. "I do think I was missed." He glanced at the other kids and said, "but not by my nephews and niece?"

Zakai said, "No, Uncle, we missed you too and love you." They rushed over to him and gave him a group hug before going back to their seats.

Andre hugged his wife and patted Breezy's head, who was wagging her tail and looking as if she, too, needed a hug.

"Alright." Andre said, "Come here, girl. Give Daddy a big hug." He stooped, giving Breezy a tight squeeze around the neck, while rubbing her head.

"Are you hungry?" Khalilah asked.

"No, I ate at the airport before boarding the flight."

"Are you sure?" she asked. "I can make you a burger and I made your favourite salad."

"I'm fine." He looked at the kids and couldn't believe they were growing up so fast. It seemed only a short time since they'd brought them home from the hospital and now they were asking questions that caused him and his wife, both with engineering degrees, to pause and think before answering.

Fidge's voice interrupted his thought. "Dad, do you know about this thing they call a cloud that it is not the same thing as the cloud in the sky?"

"Yes, I do," he replied, "but tell me how you all got to this topic at sleepover night. I thought sleepovers were for watching movies, playing video games, and eating your favorite foods and snacks."

"We did all that, but Amar sent us some videos of some old people doing weird dance moves. We were wondering where those were kept for so long and if we can keep our own videos that we create until we get old like you," Beng said.

Andre, pretending to be hurt frowned as he asked, "Are you really saying I am old?"

"No, not really, Uncle. Gremaa and Granddad are old. You are kinda old," Amar said, as he tried to sound kind.

Andre chuckled. "I think I will join you all and listen to your aunt. I know I will learn something new too."

Beng looked over at his father, "Right, Dad. We are waiting on the questions you are going to ask Mom." He couldn't imagine his father was serious about having questions like they did, because he was convinced his dad knew everything. *But, maybe Dad has heard about the cloud but doesn't know much about it since he builds bridges and big buildings, and Mom works with computers in the cloud!*

Beng settled in his chair and eagerly awaited his dad's questions, which never came. Khalilah started by asking them if they now understood that it took lots of people to process raw data.

Amar said, "I do, but I am not sure who they are, except for the big data engineers."

"Remember, we talked earlier about the phones we used before you were born, and how they were big but could not do most of the things our current phones are doing now."

"Yes," said Rachel.

"That's because new technologies being developed the big data engineers and other professionals have enabled our phones to do so much more today. They have also created new jobs for computer engineers like me."

Khalilah thought it a good time to introduce the concept of STEM. "Speaking of new jobs," she continued. "You should know the term STEM."

"Oh, here we go again," Amar said. "I bet it's not the thing the flowers grow on!"

Khalilah laughed.

"Auntie, what does STEM mean? I'm confused as I thought only flowers and drinking glasses have stems," Zakai asked, scratching his head.

Fidge said, "First, cloud, now STEM. Mom, are you sure you are not tricking us?"

Andre laughed as he looked sympathetically at his wife. Holding up his hands in a gesture of surrender, he mouthed silently "Sorry, you are on your own."

"Not at all, Fidge. I would not try to trick you. This is serious. Please remember the word STEM as you'll be hearing it a lot." Khalilah said. "Once you get to high school, you'll be hearing about this STEM which stands for science, technology, engineering, and mathematics. When I was in high school, we simply called it the sciences."

"Man, these words! People need help choosing names because they are just confusing us kids. Think about it, Uncle, cloud and STEM, isn't it kinda crazy?" Amar asked.

Andre thought about giving a frivolous response but changed his mind when he glanced at his wife and saw how serious she was.

"You know, Amar, you are correct. These words can be confusing. Sure, if there is a way to get them changed so they are less confusing, that would be great. For now, though, I think it is better to know the different meanings and uses as you focus on your aunt's explanations," Andre urged.

"Agreed, Uncle," Amar said, nodding.

STEM OR STEM

Khalilah felt the children's silence was her cue to get the discussion back on track. "Let us talk about one of the new careers in STEM. You all know what a career is?"

"Yes," they replied in unison.

Beng reminded his mom that both she and his dad had talked with them many times about careers.

"Great," Khalilah said, "I'm glad you all remember, as we will now talk in more detail about a new career in STEM. Big data engineering or BDE for short. The BDE is the person who works on raw data, so it becomes useful to us. It is the BDE's work that allows us to place orders, pay bills, get information from Alexa, watch videos, and play video games online in easy ways."

"And this person is really called a big data engineer?" Fidge repeated. "Why such a name?"

"First, remember we talked earlier about the amount of data that is generated from using your phones, computers, social media, and video games? Zakai had said it was like a kazillion, which as we said earlier is not an exact number but it's pretty big. Think of a number so large, that are the number of steps it would take to walk to the moon and back many times."

Rachel wondered how anyone could walk to the moon. She knew people had walked on the moon but never heard of them walking to it. She raised her hand. "Auntie, how can I imagine all of that when it's impossible?"

Khalilah laughed. "It's not meant to be real; you just have to imagine it."

Rachel felt a bit flustered but didn't ask a follow up question.

"Are you okay Rachel?" Khalilah asked.

"Yes, I am Aunty, let's go on."

Andre gave another example since Rachel still seemed flustered: "Imagine how many ants are on our entire planet. Does that image give you a sense of how big the data in a cloud is?"

"Uncle," Amar exclaimed, "are you serious?"

"Yes, I am," he replied.

They all looked at him, puzzled.

"Of course, the number can't be exact, but it is estimated to be about twenty quadrillion or twenty thousand trillion. The amount of data that big data engineers analyze is even larger."

Khalilah continued. "There are many new careers that many students are not yet aware of. Schools and corporations who will need to hire these persons are doing a lot to bring information to students. They also encourage them to get into scientific fields. These are the jobs coming on stream now and in the near future as technology becomes even more advanced and we do more and more with our tiny phones. More online ordering, calling Uber, playing games, sending, and receiving messages and videos.

You name it." She looked around the table to be sure they were still listening, and they were.

"Now, if you all remember, it was the question about how you store and retrieve videos after long periods of time that led to this conversation."

"Yes," Beng scratched his head.

"All we discussed earlier are part of the solution. People who understand science and how to best use it to make the world easier to manage. The physical computers that are connected using miles of cables and wireless technology (Wi-Fi) is another part of the solution. These cables and Wi-Fi connect computers from different locations around the world, enabling them to communicate and work together at the same time. Some of these cables are run under the seas and oceans and back on land to where the computers are installed. Satellite Towers that bounce signals are built to connect data at these centers so your games and other gadgets in our house can be connected by cables, both wired and wireless."

"Yes," Fidge noted. "Like our internet connection. They are all over the house and it took the cable technician a long time to install them all before we could use the internet."

"Correct," Khalilah continued "but the cables under the sea are bigger and carry much more information. This allows the computers in different countries to communicate with each other quickly."

"Whoa! No way!" Rachel said. "I have a million questions, Auntie. How are cables kept down there? How come big fish like sharks do not eat these cables and how do the cables know where to send everybody's information that we type and need? This is crazy!"

Khalilah laughed. "Very good questions, Rachel, but we can't answer them all today. For now, can we agree to talk about the job of the big data engineer and at the next sleepover we can discuss the cables?"

"Amen and amen," Zakai said. "My head hurts. This is all very difficult, and we need to end this class so we can visit Geemaa then go to the mall." This was like a discussion in a school class. His aunt knew a lot and explained things just like his favourite teacher, Mr Fernandez.

TOO MANY ENGINEERS

ndre looked at his wife and out on the garden and felt a sense of calm and peace. Khalilah was so good with the children. Her patience and understanding always made him feel she was the better parent and he wondered how he would've handled this situation were he in her place. Not quite as patiently he imagined. He'd certainly made the right choice for a life partner.

Rachel walked across the porch to where her uncle stood. She looked up at him and said, "Can I ask you a question, Uncle Andre?"

"Sure, what's up?"

"If the big data person is an engineer, why can't you do it? Aren't you and Auntie engineers?"

She's on point, Andre thought. "Yes, Aunt Kay and I are both engineers but there are many types of engineers who are trained and who specialize in different things. I am a civil engineer. Uncle Grayson is a chemical engineer, Your cousin Jaylen is a structural engineer who designs roads, bridges, and dams. Auntie Kristina is a civil engineer like me. We all do different kinds of jobs.

Beng heard his dad, stood up from his chair, then asked, "Why can't we see the things the big data engineer builds like we see bridges, paints and buildings of other engineers?" Beng thought about all the drawings he had seen in his father's office and on his computer. He also saw his mom's design of computer equipment and networks. This big data engineer didn't seem to do anything like that. He needed to ask one more question: "Mom, why can't we see drawings and pictures of what the BDE does?"

"You can," Khalilah replied. "I promise to add it to the list of things to explain on our next sleep over. For now, focus on understanding this new career that many kids do not know about. If you get interested in STEM you'll begin to understand many things about how the world works."

Andre nodded in agreement.

"Isn't this all so exciting?" Khalilah said.

"I would say interesting, Mom. Exciting may be pushing your luck." Beng laughed.

"Okay, you may be right," Khalilah admitted, "but there are a few more things I would like to share." Realizing she could not answer all questions in a simple way, she told them they would also get more detailed answers when they were in high school.

"Auntie, if we are finished can we go to the mall now. That would be great."

Amar thought the discussion was good, but he had promised some friends they would meet at the mall to check out the new games at the video arcade and he was ready to go. His other cousins, who were not at the sleepover, had also been given

permission to go with him to the Mall and were meeting them there at 3:00 p.m. . He didn't want to be late. If the older kids got there before them, they'd stayed on the new machines until they felt like giving them up, which was usually past his curfew.

"Well, well," Khalilah said. "Now you all want me to rush. Remember you came to me with your questions about video storage and a cloud. Guess you never thought asking where videos are stored and accessed from the internet would have such an involved discussion?"

"We know, Auntie," Rachel said in a tired voice.

"I do admire your curiosity and questions which are very good. Your knowledge of these topics will certainly help when you get to high school," Khalilah told them.

"I was just joking, Auntie. Let's continue. I'm still curious," Rachel assured her.

"Beng, do you remember that we are to meet Ashley, Simone, and Matt at the mall at 3'oclock to check out the new machine at the arcade?" Amar asked.

"Yes. Mom is it okay of we go to the Mall now? We can stop by the computer store before we meet our friends."

"Do you still have questions?"

"Yes...but they can wait until the next sleep over. You did great, Mom."

"Yes. You did great Auntie, and we can't wait for the next sleepover.

"Thanks, kids, "Khalilah continued. So, everyone get ready and be in the van in five minutes.

On the way to the Mall the kids began talking. "I know who is not going to be a BDE," Zakai said, "Me."

"Why?" Beng asked.

"Because math and science are hard." Zakai remembered only too well that he'd gotten a B-minus on his last math test, after he had studied so hard. If this STEM stuff was required to be a BDE, he was beginning to feel like this big data engineering was not what he wanted to do when he grew up.

Fidge said, "I don't think I'll be one either. I prefer to draw and make anime. I don't need to be a math and science genius to become an animator," she bragged. "My teacher says I am very good at drawing things and people." She pulled out her phone, found pictures from her anime class and passed it around. "Told you. I'm good. So, I know who a big data engineer won't be! Yes, me!" she said, looking very pleased with herself.

"Not everyone will become a big data engineer, but it's good to learn about them careers and have an understanding of." Khalilah said.

She reflected on her journey to becoming a computer network engineer. Her parents did not know much about computers, or the careers associated with them. Their dream was that she would become a successful lawyer. In her first year of university, a professor, Dr Jay Shah, told her about the new emerging careers associated with computers. She was skeptical at first, but after discussing it further with him, she decided to try computer networking. The rest was history. Her parents were not pleased at first, in fact they were annoyed and confused, but finally decided to support her decision. Now they were very proud of her accomplishments.

"Well, I might become a BDE, but I am still not as good as Amar," Zakai said.

Do not despair," Khalilah interjected. "There are new ways of teaching math which are proving to be successful."

"I'm not that good anyway," Amar said. "One thing is for sure though, is that if I become a BDE I am going to petition for a name changes for cloud and stem."

"But you know we use math and sciences in everyday life to solve problems. For example, when you are assembling a new toy. The engineers make life simpler by including instruction manuals, so you don't have to think about it. When you receive the box with the parts and manual of instructions, do you try to put the toy together without first reading the instructions?" Andre added.

"Sometimes," Zakai said, sheepishly.

"Is that why when Beng got the Harry Potter LEGO kit he had such a hard time putting it together? He did not read the instructions first," Fidge said, pointing at him as she laughed.

Beng gave her a thumbs down to express his disapproval. "Most times, I try putting toys and games together without reading the instructions. I think that if I can put the pieces together without the manuals it means I'm as smart as the people who built them." He hesitated, as if rethinking, "But I find when I think about it first and read the instructions then it is easier to assemble"

"Dad," Fidge touched Andre's arm, "why do we have to read instructions? Sometimes, they are confusing."

Andre blinked as he refocused on the discussion. Last he'd heard was the need to read instructions first. "Yes, reading instructions before assembling anything is always best. Let's see. When you got your new bike, didn't I read the instructions before trying to put it together?"

"Yes, Dad," Fidge said, "but doing all that reading can slow you down."

"Not so sure of that," he said, "not reading the instructions could cause you to make more mistakes and take longer. Don't you think so?"

"Well, maybe," Fidge admitted.

"That is true, Uncle," Zakai said. "When I tried to assemble my Gravity Maze, it took me a little longer because, at first, I didn't look at the instructions."

Fidge tugged at Andre's arm, asking, "Dad, there must be some things you can put together without reading the manual?"

"Like we have been saying, Fidge, the manuals are there to help and make your task easier. The manufacturers do recommend you use them," he replied.

Khalilah added, "Can we agree, the lesson here is we need to slow down when there is a problem or situation, think about it, then try to solve it. If you have instructions, make sure you use them. This is one of the key things a big data engineer must learn to do very well in order to take raw data and organize it as instructed by the algorithms into usable data."

"Okay, Auntie, I understand we need to read and follow instructions. I guess after going to school and practicing we'll understand everything else in due time."

"Yes, Amar. And then when get your certification you can make a lot of money."

AT THE MALL

They reached the Mall and the children piled out of the SUV.

"We'll pick up in two or three hours, and please stick together," Andre said to the kids.

"Three please, Dad."

"And while you're playing those games think of how the BDE is making your life fun." Khalilah said.

"Whee, we sure learned a lot today. I am glad we got to the Mall by the time Auntie brought up certification. I don't even know what that is."

"Remember when Jamil worked for your uncle Andre?" Beng asked.

"Yes," Amar recalled. *He remembered Jamil well. They had met at a soccer game they all attended a few months before. Jamil knew a lot about the game and seemed to have impressed the grownups. Rachel told him that she played soccer for school. He really liked that and told them about his time in high school and university where he was a star soccer player.*

"Why aren't you playing for the Major League?" Rachel had asked sarcastically.

Jamil explained he had fully intended to join the league but had to give up playing when he broke his leg and was not able to play well since then. He shared how very unhappy he was but got over his sadness with help from his friends, family, and coaches. Now, he coached young people, like her, to improve their skills.

"After, he completed his university studies to coach he needed to be certified. He worked for one year and did so well, he is now hired permanently," Beng said. "I've heard the certification story already from mom."

As the boys rounded the corner, they saw their friend and cousins coming toward them.

"Hey guys." Amar said. "lets hurry to the gaming spot before the bigger guys get there. We'll tell you all we learned today about gaming."

ABOUT THE BOOK SERIES

Young children today as early as three years old or even younger are considered technology natives. Exposed to its use from an earlier age, they are far more fluent that the average adult and now have new options open to them for future career choices. Parents and teachers too must become fluent in non-traditional career options if they are to guide our youngsters through the maze of new careers technology has created. As parents and teachers, becoming familiar with the pro and cons of technology will be beneficial as you guide young minds toward the tasks that will be rooted in the technology of the future.

CPSIA information can be obtained
at www.ICGtesting.com
Printed in the USA
JSHW011753090523
41459JS00005B/27

9 781959 811107